POCKET PRAYERS
for WOMEN

Finding
Angels
When You Need Them

Love you,
Winnie
4/10/14

Publications International, Ltd.

Author: Marie D. Jones

Additional contributors: Anne Broyles, Nancy Parker Brummet, Pam Campbell, Elaine Wright Colvin, Elaine Creasman, Christine A. Dallman, June Eaton, Lain Chroust Ehmann, Margaret Ann Huffman, Jennifer Huston, Randy Petersen, Ellen F. Pill, Carol McAdoo Rehme, Carol Smith, Carol Stigger, Anna Trimiew, Natalie Walker Whitlock, Gary Wilde, Kelly Womer

Cover Art: Shutterstock.com

Interior Art: Getty, Shutterstock.com

Angels Are Everywhere

Humans like to feel that they are in control of their lives. But it's comforting to know that God sends his angels to guide and protect us.

Pocket Prayers for Women: Finding Angels When You Need Them is a devotional of prayers asking God to send his angels when we most need love and support. The Bible passages and inspirational quotes included help us express our love for the Lord and his heavenly hosts.

Best of all, *Pocket Prayers for Women: Finding Angels When You Need Them* is small enough to fit inside a purse or briefcase, making it easy to take advantage of the privilege of talking with God and your guardian angels every day.

Guided and Guarded

Blessed are those who trust in the Lord,
whose trust is the Lord.

Jeremiah 17:7

Dear God, I want to thank you for my guardian angel—my rock and the column I can always lean on. I may be short on trust of the people in my world sometimes, but I know that I can count on my angel to be there with love and support. I know that through your angels, you will always protect me and guide me through each day and night so that I am never truly alone. For that I am so thankful.

Watching from Above

Do they sit and watch us, these angels of which we are unaware? Do they lie on a cloud, heads on their hands, and peek at our world? I think I can see them sometimes if I look up and squint really hard. I think I can hear them sometimes—celestial murmurs that accompany our hardships and will one day lead us home.

When we are feeling alone, assailed by outside forces, unsure of which way to go, it is comforting to think of angels watching over us, providing celestial support and guidance.

Hearing God's Voice

And thine ears shall hear a word behind thee, saying, This is the way, walk ye in it, when ye turn to the right hand, and when ye turn to the left.

Isaiah 30:21 KJV

Lord, even if I don't hear your voice as audibly as Moses and others did, I can still hear it in my spirit. And how desperate I am to hear from you at certain times of my life, Lord. Today I pray you would give me ears to listen so that all the wisdom and comfort you want to send to me will come through loud and clear. Thank you for speaking to me, Lord. Amen.

The most important voice to hear is the voice of God.

Send Me an Angel

*The Lord... will send his angel with you
and make your way successful.*

Genesis 24:40

Lord, please send me an angel to
guide me and guard me, to lead
and direct me, to comfort and hold me.
Send me an angel who knows what
my heart needs most and always has
the solutions to my most challenging
problems. Send me an angel to walk
with me and hold my hand as I tread the
rocky road of life. Send me an angel soon.

*Angels help us believe in the things we
cannot see and understand the things we
can. Angels give us the faith and wisdom
to know that all things are possible.*

Home Is Where Your Heart Is

"Do not let your hearts be troubled.
Believe in God, believe also in me.
In my Father's house there are many
dwelling places."

John 14:1–2

ow blessed I am, God, to have
such a wonderful place to
call home, with such wonderful people
in my life, and to be surrounded by
such wonderful things. My home is like
heaven on earth, filled with specially
chosen angels that accompany me on
this amazing journey called life. I feel

safe, secure, and loved here, and I am so
blessed to have a place to live and dream
that brings out the best in me and all
who walk through these doors. Thank
you, God, for my beautiful home—my
little slice of heaven.

When we dwell in love and gratitude,
any place we go becomes our home.
For our true home is within us,
where our hearts live.

A Compassionate Heart

As God's chosen ones, holy and beloved,
clothe yourselves with compassion,
kindness, humility, meekness, and patience.

Colossians 3:12

*L*ord, help me to have a more compassionate heart toward those I meet today. Whether they are positive or negative in spirit, guide me to deal with each of them as I myself would want to be treated, remembering that we are all human and are all capable of our ups and downs. Have my guardian angel remind me to react from the highest place within me, not the lowest, and to strive to be as good to them as you are to me. Thank you, God.

Open My Eyes

God, help me recognize the angels in my life, especially those who come in the form of people I meet. Sometimes, I forget to smile at a stranger or exchange a pleasantry with a store clerk, yet they, too, could be angels. Remind me to keep my eyes and my heart open to the angels that are part of my daily life, always ready to offer a loving word or a kind gesture.

Life is short and we have never too much time for gladdening the hearts of those who are traveling the dark journey with us. Oh be swift to love, make haste to be kind.

—Henri Frederic Amiel

A Prayer for the Brokenhearted

Hope deferred makes the heart sick,
but a desire fulfilled is a tree of life.

Proverbs 13:12

*L*oving God,
My heart is breaking and I don't know what to do. Please send me an angel to light my way and help me see past the dark clouds of despair to a day when the sun will shine again. Please heal my heart so that I can experience true love with the special someone you have chosen just for me. Thank you. Amen.

Restore My Soul

For God alone my soul waits in silence,
  for my hope is from him. He alone is
my rock and my salvation, my fortress;
    I shall not be shaken.

Psalm 62:5–6

Grace of my heart, I turn to you
when I am feeling lost and alone.
You restore me with strength and
hope and the courage to face a new
day. You bless me with joy and angels
who comfort me through trials and
tribulations. You direct my thoughts,
guide my actions, and temper my words.
You give me the patience and kindness
I need to be good. Grace of my heart,
I turn to you. Amen.

Furry Angels

The righteous know the needs
of their animals…

Proverbs 12:10

God, how I adore my pets, for they love me unconditionally. Like furry little angels, they love me even at my worst and are my constant and faithful companions through life's ups and downs. Every pet I've ever been blessed with has taught me so much about being in the present moment and taking life as it is and as it comes. They have been some of my greatest teachers, and I am so thankful for the creatures you have sent my way. May I learn to love as they do: without hesitation and with a wide-open heart. Amen.

*Thank you, God, for all the animals
that have helped us feel closer to you
and your creation. Keep them safe, these
trusted innocents that calm our lives and
show us love. Help them find their way
home if they are lost. Help them hear the
voices of those who will care for them.
Protect them from every unsafe place.*

Birds of a Feather

Hope does not disappoint us,
because God's love has been poured
into our hearts through the Holy Spirit
that has been given to us.

Romans 5:5

Troubles, dear Lord, have cast me loose from assumptions and certainties, and I am bobbing like a rudderless boat on a stormy sea. When all hope seems gone, I spot doves on the horizon. Doves like those you sent Noah to assure him the storm was nearly over. Doves in the phone calls from friends; in the smile of a neighbor; in the wisdom of a caregiver or counselor; in good laughs or hearty cleansing tears; in the flash of a new idea, a goal, a dream. I recognize landmarks now and can see my way through the storm, guided by your love-winged messengers.

You'll See It
When You Believe It!

Have you believed because you have seen me? Blessed are those who have not seen and yet have come to believe.

John 20:29

*G*od, thank you for the little things that restore my faith and make me believe in the goodness of life again. I can sometimes get stuck in negative thinking, but I know I can count on my loved ones to help dig me out of any rut, no matter how deep and hopeless it might seem.

The ignorant say they will believe in angels only when they see them. The wise understand that they will see angels only when they believe in them.

18

Faith in Love

O God, who art the truth, make me one with Thee in continual love! I am weary often to read and hear many things. In Thee is all that I desire and long for. Let all teachers hold their peace; let all creatures be silent in Thy sight; speak to me alone.

—Thomas à Kempis, *The Imitation of Christ*

When confusion sets in, and when there is too much advice coming from too many places, don't forget God, his wisdom, and his love.

This Too Shall Pass

Rejoice in hope, be patient in suffering,
persevere in prayer.

Romans 12:12

Lord, we both know that patience is not one of my strong suits, but I feel so tense and anxious when things don't happen right away. I pray for peace and understanding as I wait for things to change. As I deal with what lies ahead, send me an angel to watch over me and keep my head on straight and my heart in the right place. I know miracles are right around the corner. I just need a little extra loving care right now until I get there.

Lead the Way!

Heavenly Father, I think about the moments in my life when you have changed me. I think about the words that gave me a new perspective—a new direction. I think about the angels who stepped into my life and were used by you to show me the way. I think about all these things, and I am grateful. I think about all these moments, and I am filled with confidence that you have led me on my way.

Life is beyond our control. That is precisely why angels guard us and guide us.

A Grateful Prayer for My Support System

Some friends play at friendship but a true friend sticks closer than one's nearest kin.

Proverbs 18:24

Lord, you've given me a great team of helpers, and I'm exceedingly thankful. Where would I be without them? They seem to know my needs before I do, and they jump to meet them. I know you've instilled in them the gifts of caring, encouragement, hospitality, and healing, and they're using those gifts as you intended—to show your love to others, including me. For that, I am thankful to you and to them.

But there's not much I can do to pay them back, Lord. They'd probably refuse a reward anyway. So I ask that you shower them with blessings, just as they have blessed me. Give them joy and peace in rich supply, and let your love continue to flow to them, through them, and within them. Amen.

> *We cannot part with our friends;*
> *we cannot let our angels go.*
> —Ralph Waldo Emerson

The Kindness of Strangers

Do not neglect to show hospitality to strangers, for by doing that some have entertained angels without knowing it.

Hebrews 13:2

God, we are so often buried in our cell phones and electronic gadgets that we rarely talk to strangers anymore. How rare it is these days that we stop and say hello, offer a smile, or engage in small talk. I pray that I may never ignore the kindness of the strangers who reach out to me and that I may reach out to them as well, offering what little joy I can to help make their day a bit brighter. Lord, let me be an angel to a stranger today. Amen.

The Gift Is in the Present

So do not worry about tomorrow, for tomorrow will bring worries of its own. Today's trouble is enough for today.

Matthew 6:34

God, I have always thought that my guardian angels were living things, like friends and family and my pets. But lately I've been receiving guidance everywhere I look: in a quote I see on a social-networking site or an email a friend sends with an inspiring image. Sometimes I'll open a book and turn to just the right passage that I need to read. And then I realize that angels are everywhere when I allow myself to see them. Thank you, God!

Your Heavenly Embrace

Though I cannot see you, angel dear,
I know that you are there.
Though I cannot hear you speak,
I sense you loud and clear.
For in my heart I recognize
The pattern of your call.
And in your wings I've found
A gentle place to fall.

Should I attempt to see you, angel dear,
I know that I will fail.
Should I attempt to pin you down,
I know I won't prevail.
For in my soul I've come to know
Your presence is discerned.
And through my faith I understand
That mercy must be earned.

If ever I am lonely, angel dear,
I know you're close at hand.
If ever I am frightened,
I know that by me you will stand.
For in the quiet of the night,
I sense God's loving grace
And rest in the peaceful comfort
Of your heavenly embrace.

Love finds us all, one way or another.
Love gives us reason and hope.
Love wraps its wings around our weakness
and carries us all the way home.

Seeking Your Angels

For he will command his angels
concerning you to guard you in all
your ways. On their hands they will bear
you up, so that you will not dash
your foot against a stone.

Psalm 91:11–12

We're seldom, if ever, truly "in this alone." In the midst of trouble, we may feel dreadfully lonely, but healing rarely comes without a little or a lot of help from outside—from those people in our lives who act as our earthly guardian angels extending God's help and love.

Seeking your personal angels might literally mean going out and looking for the right person to help with your particular problem. Just as often, though, it means learning to recognize the angels who are already knocking at your door. Pain and sorrow can blind us to the compassionate friends nearby who are eager and able to help us on the road to recovery. If you're ready to seek healing, take a good look around. Your earthly angel might be standing right in front of you.

Recognizing the presence of angels around you can feel like walking from the shadows into the warmth of sunshine. Suddenly, you feel the nourishment that comes from someone taking the time to look out for you and you alone.

Seeing God in Others

Bear with one another and, if anyone has
a complaint against another, forgive each
other; just as the Lord has forgiven you, so
you also must forgive.

Colossians 3:13

Lord, I don't know if I thank you
often enough for the people you
put into my life, and so today I don't
want to do anything else before I lift
my heartfelt gratitude up to you. In
your wisdom, you know how much we
need family and friends near and far to
encourage us, to come beside us when we
are lonely, to simply provide a reflection
of you, of your love and forgiveness.
Thank you that I can see glimpses of you

in others, Lord. May someone else see you
in my eyes today. Amen.

> *Blest be the tie that binds*
> *Our hearts in Christian love;*
> *The fellowship of kindred minds*
> *Is like to that above.*
> —John Fawcett

Thanks for Understanding

Great is our Lord, and abundant in power;
his understanding is beyond measure.

Psalm 147:5

Dear God, I'm sorry if I get frustrated or upset with my guardian angel these days. I know I must not always be the easiest person to be a guardian angel for. It's just that I'm having a hard time right now. And I sometimes forget how truly blessed I am and how good you are to me. I hope you and my guardian angel will be patient with me, and help see me through to better times. Thank you for understanding.

Protector of All

Cast your cares on the Lord and
he will sustain you; he will never let
the righteous be shaken.

Psalm 55:22 NIV

*L*ord, you send your angels to us
each day when we need them
most. We thank you for the protection,
reassurance, and blessings they offer in
your name. Please continue to shower us
with these daily reminders of your great
love for us and keep us safely tucked
beneath the shadow of angel wings.

*When life seems darkest and we feel lost
and alone, that's when we are surrounded
by angels who care for us. All we need to
do is open our hearts to see them reaching
out to us with love.*

33

God's Merciful Messengers

Then Peter... said,
"Now I am sure that the Lord has sent
his angel and rescued me..."

Acts 12:11

Heavenly Father, thank you for your holy angels, both those in heaven and those here on earth. They make life more bearable in times of trouble, and they add to our joy in good times. Keep us always in your sight, Lord. When we stumble, send your merciful messengers to pick us up. When we are lost, send them to light the way home.

God sends his angels to hold us up so we don't stumble in the darkness.

Thank You for My Angels

Dear God,
I am so thankful for the angels of light who guide my journey and for the angels of wisdom who whisper to me what I need to know.

I am so thankful for the angels of joy who remind me of the happiness in my life.

And I am so thankful for the guardian angel who is always with me, keeping me safe. Amen.

Spanning Heaven and Earth

Halos and wings and harps and strings. Is that an angel's world? Are their streets made of gold, adorned with clockless cathedrals, surrounding a celestial park? Not for guardian angels. These are the beings spanning the beauty of heaven and the sometimes harsh reality of earth. They are the ones sweeping through town at the speed of humans, following their charges who are full of stubborn will and free spirit. They are the ones standing watch over lives undaunted. And whether or not we acknowledge their presence, they remain by our sides—always.

Promises Kept

For the Lord will not forsake his people;
he will not abandon his heritage.

Psalm 94:14

Heavenly Father, thank you for the times you've intervened in my life through angels. They bring the reality of your caring heart into the reality of my days. By them, you remind me that you have promised never to leave me nor forsake me. Thank you for the comfort you give through the angels you send.

I call upon God for comfort and solace,
and he sends me angels to answer
my plea. They gently mend my broken
heart, and I am at peace in the world
and one with heaven.

Finding Home

*I will seek the lost, and I will bring back
the strayed, and I will bind up the injured,
and I will strengthen the weak.*

Ezekiel 34:16

Confusion is directing my thoughts.
My mind loyally follows its erratic
demands and becomes increasingly
lost and frustrated. I need a sign to
orient myself and to find my way out
of this turmoil. Find me, Lord, for I am
wandering in the wilderness of my own
mind, heading deeper and deeper into
despair. *Where are you?* I call. And then
I realize that by describing my lostness,
you show me where I am and how to
return home.

O God, our help in ages past,
our hope for years to come,
our shelter from the stormy blast, and our
eternal home.

Under the shadow of your throne
your saints have dwelt secure;
sufficient is your arm alone, and our
defense is sure.

—Isaac Watts,
"O God, Our Help in Ages Past"

What a Wonderful World!

They shall again live beneath my shadow,
they shall flourish as a garden;
they shall blossom like a vine,
their fragrance shall be like
the wine of Lebanon.

Hosea 14:7

Sometimes, I wake up in the morning, Lord, and the first I do is think about all the things on my To Do list and stress about bills and family and work. But then I hear the gentle call of a bird or feel the breeze on my skin, and I realize I am so blessed to be alive! The world is such a magical place, filled with beauty and love. When I set my focus on the beauty and love around me, the stressful things lose their power, and I realize that life is about so much more than just plodding through each day. It's about living and loving and being in a world full of miracles. Thank you, Lord, for such a wonderful world that's teeming with angels in the form of birds and breezes and beautiful things!

Life is what you make of it.
It can be a lovely garden or
a bed of weeds. Look for the beauty
in everything and you will find it.

An Abundance of Angels

Bless the Lord, O you his angels,
you mighty ones who do his bidding,
obedient to his spoken word.

Psalm 103:20

*L*ord, I know that you simply cannot be everywhere at once, so you made angels to help you spread your loving grace upon the earth. Thank you for blessing my life with an abundance of angels in the form of friends and family members who love and care for me. They fill my life with joy and give me wings to follow my dreams.

Take My Hand

Behold, I send an Angel before thee, to keep thee in the way, and to bring thee into the place which I have prepared.

Exodus 23:20 KJV

Father God, teach me to trust your protection. It's so hard sometimes to find my way home. The nights get dark. The clouds hide the stars. If I could learn to hold the hands of your angels, I know you would lead me all the way.

Angels are everywhere, waiting to help us through the hardest of times. All we need to do is ask for their help and believe we will receive it.

An Angel for All Seasons

*L*oving God, help us sense your angelic messengers whenever, wherever, and however they come to us. In the darkness of winter, the brightness of spring, the abundance of summer, and the transitions of autumn, may we expect to be visited by your heavenly beings. And when these visits happen, may our eyes be open and our gratitude heartfelt.

There is no one time or place
When angels can appear.
They come when needed,
Filled with grace
To those who God holds dear.

Surrounded by Angels

*Be strong and bold; have no fear or dread
of them, because it is the Lord your God
who goes with you; he will not fail you
or forsake you.*

Deuteronomy 31:6

The angels in my life are often very familiar in form. When I was sick, I thought an angel touched my forehead with a cool cloth, but it was my mother. When I was afraid, I thought an angel comforted me, but it was my brother. When I was alone, I thought an angel sat beside me, but it was my friend. Looking back, I think I was right the first time.

*The unlikeliest people harbor halos
underneath their hats.*

Help Me Do God's Work

Heavenly Father, just for today, please keep my eyes open, my hands willing, and my heart eager to help everyone in need who crosses my path—even if the need is as small as an encouraging smile and even if it requires a sacrifice of time and resources. Just for today, God. With your guidance, I have faith that, day by day, I can help more, give more, and be an earthly angel to those in need.

When we find ourselves the agents of God's goodness to others in the course of a day, we are participating in the work of angels.

With God All Things Are Possible

God is faithful, and he will not let you be tested beyond your strength, but with the testing he will also provide the way out so that you may be able to endure it.

1 Corinthians 10:13

These hard times help me see with new eyes, Lord. Despite my tears, I see more clearly your tender mercies, my great need for your presence in my life, and the angels I had overlooked or would never have otherwise seen. Sometimes I think that I'm not strong enough to handle the tests life throws at me, but I know that with you and your angels by my side, I can do anything. Thank you for opening my eyes and healing my heart.

Ripples of Love

His master said to him, "Well done, good and trustworthy slave; you have been trustworthy in a few things, I will put you in charge of many things; enter into the joy of your master."

Matthew 25:23

Bless us, O Lord, as we toss ourselves, unique talents and all, into the stream of life, as if called to make ripples wherever we are. Use us to spread love, which is a gift that keeps making ever-widening circles eventually reaching even those stranded on the edge of the shore.

God's Perfect Love

If you listen carefully you may hear,
  An angel whispering softly in
your ear,
With a voice like the coo of a dove,
Whispering of God's perfect love.

*The height to which love exalts is
unspeakable. Love unites us to God.
Love covers a multitude of sins.
Love beareth all things, is long-suffering in
all things. There is nothing base, nothing
arrogant in love. . . . By love have all the
elect of God been made perfect.*

—Clement of Rome

Believe in Miracles

Are not all angels ministering spirits sent to serve those who will inherit salvation?

Hebrews 1:14 NIV

*L*ord, in times of weakness and doubt, help me remember that you are always capable of miracles. Keep me ever alert for visits from the angels you send to protect and guide me. May I receive them with a joyous and grateful heart and then pass on the blessings to others who need their comfort. Amen.

My New Beginning

Today is my new beginning,
The past is over and done,
However I got to this point,
From here I can only move on.
Though the road ahead may be rocky,
And the future I cannot see,
I'll walk with my head held high,
With angels on each side of me.
Today is my new beginning,
And as I depart, I will pray,
That God will bless my journey,
And guide me each step of the way.

*A new beginning, like the breath of an
angel, makes the air a little sweeter and
the world seem full of hope.*

Bless All the Little Children

Children are a gift from God;
they are his reward.

Psalm 127:3 TLB

I want to pray for the children in my life, Father. They're so innocent, and this world can sometimes be a harsh place. Thank you for assigning them a special place in your care and for giving their guardian angels direct access to you at all times. Be with them today and protect them—heart, mind, body, and soul. I know they will thrive in your love.

Guide Me, Lord

"In your steadfast love you led the people whom you redeemed; you guided them by your strength to your holy abode."

Exodus 15:13

Help me be open to your guidance, Lord, however it comes. When you speak to me in the words of a friend, open my ears. When you hold me in the embrace of a family member, let me feel your gentle touch. And when you come to me in the almost imperceptible rush of angels' wings, alert my senses to your presence.

Riding on the wings of angels, you can see your life from a distance and let go of the small and unimportant concerns that hold you down.

Light and Free

I will exult in the God of my salvation.
God, the Lord, is my strength; he makes my
feet like the feet of a deer, and makes me
tread upon the heights.

Habakkuk 3:18–19

God, I feel so light and free today. Everything is coming together, and the way ahead seems so clear. I've had so many issues lately with relationships and family, finances and work, and for a while I felt trapped in a fog. I love these mornings when the sun is shining and the birds are singing and all is well in my world again. I thank you for all the blessings you have given me and those yet to come. I know life will once again throw rocks in my path, but it's times like this when I am reminded that not only can I handle them, I can also learn from each and every rock and become a happier, stronger person as a result. Thank you, God, for being the wind beneath my wings.

Isn't it funny how when we stop and take the time to recognize all the good in our lives, it leads to more and more good? Blessings beget more blessings, and gratitude begets more to be grateful for!

The Spirit Within

*Do you not know that you are God's temple
and that God's Spirit dwells in you?*

1 Corinthians 3:16

Imagine, if you can…
A love so deep it swallows fear,
A love so wide it embraces pain,
A love so high it humbles pride,
A love so thick it absorbs all sin.
Imagine, but don't stop there!
Come with your fear,
Your pain,
Your pride,
Your sin.
Come to God who loves—
Purely, perfectly, precisely—
You.

He Will Be Found

*Ask, and it will be given you; search, and
you will find; knock, and the door will be
opened for you. For everyone who asks
receives, and everyone who searches finds,
and for everyone who knocks, the door will
be opened.*

Matthew 7:7–8

Lord God Almighty, how honored
we are that you allow yourself
to be found by those who honestly seek
you! You are all powerful, all knowing,
all seeing, and yet you openly welcome
all those who come looking for you. I
seek your involvement in everything
I do today, Lord. Thank you for your
accessibility to us. Amen.

Speak to Me, Lord

Open my eyes that I may see
wonderful things...

Psalm 119:18 NIV

O Lord, we give thanks for your presence, which greets us each day in the guise of a friend, a work of nature, or a story from a stranger. We are reminded through these messengers in our times of deepest need that you are indeed watching over us. Lord, we have known you in the love and care of a friend, who envelops us and keeps us company in our despair. When we observe the last morning glory stretching faithfully to receive what warmth is left in the chilly sunshine, we are heartened and inspired to do the same. When we are hesitant to speak up and then read in the newspaper a story of courage and controversy, we find our voice lifted and strengthened by your message in black-and-white type. Lord, we are grateful receivers of all the angelic messages that surround us every day.

*Angels do the work of love—
love around us, love within us,
love compelling us, and love igniting us.*

When I Picture an Angel

Suddenly an angel of the Lord appeared and a light shone…

Acts 12:7

When I think of angels, I think of floating, celestial beings. I think of angels as beings who have only good thoughts, never bad. I see them surrounded by an eternal glow and always pleasant and completely centered. I picture them with such a sense of purpose, so connected to their reason for being that they never lose their way. I see angels as the kind of beings that I would like to be.

Let Me Be an Angel

*For this light within you produces only
what is good and right and true.*

Ephesians 5:9 NLT

God in heaven, let me be an angel
to someone today. Just as you have
blessed my life with people who love
and cherish me, let me be a light of love
that shines upon someone who needs me.
I have received the gift of angels, now
allow me to give and be one in return.

*If you want to be an angel for another
person, you don't need wings and a
halo—just a loving attitude. Being aware
of other people's needs, fears, dreams, and
heartaches, you can reach out as a loving
presence. You don't need to solve their
problems—you just need to offer yourself.*

Angel Friends

I believe in angels.
They're around me every day,
I see them in a mother's touch
And in a child at play.

I see them in a neighbor's wave
And in an old friend's call,
In a martyr's heroic deed
And in a favor small.

I've heard one in a friend's "hello"
And in a newborn's cry,
In the rustle of the leaves
And in a lullaby.

They're in a loved one's legacy
And in a young child's might,
They're in the colors of the sky
And in a starry night.

I've seen one in a stranger's smile
And in a lover's glance,
In an act of selflessness
And in a second chance.

I see them in a brother's arms
And in a sister's care,
I hear them in a baby's laugh
And in a small child's prayer.

Yes, I believe in angels,
And I know that they are true,
Messengers and guardians,
Angel friends like you.

Staying Nearby

Cast all your anxiety on him because
he cares for you.

1 Peter 5:7 NIV

can do it myself, I protest, but,
O God, I know it's not true. Open
me to your limitless love, which is found
in the skillful caring of those who know
firsthand my present trouble. They bring
your message home and I feel you close—
as close as angel wings beating gently
upon my stubborn loneliness.

Angels find us, not only when we need
them most, but also when we think
we are fine on our own.

Relinquishing Control

And when we cried unto the Lord,
he heard our voice, and sent an angel,
and hath brought us forth…

Numbers 20:16 KJV

God, help me to accept the help I need and to give up my stubborn need to control the outcome of every situation. Show me that sometimes my will is not always for the best, and help me see that you send us guiding angels in the form of other humans. Amen.

Angels do not change your mind;
they wait patiently until you do.

Finding Light

In my distress I cried unto the Lord,
and he heard me.

Psalm 120:1 KJV

*L*ord, I know that doubts and confusion don't come from you. On days when everything I know to be true is challenged—and I feel as if I'm walking through a fog that won't lift—be my source of truth and light. Bring me back to complete trust in you.

Lighten our darkness, Lord, we pray; and in your mercy defend us from all perils and dangers of this night; for the love of your only Son, our Savior Jesus Christ. Amen.

—"An Evening Prayer"

Worthwhile Waiting

I wait for the Lord, my soul waits,
and in his word I hope.

Psalm 130:5

Why is it so hard for me to wait, Lord? I know you see my frustration at even the slightest delay in accomplishing my plans for the day. From your perspective, I must seem like an impatient child. Bathe me in your word, Lord. Calm my desperate mind with your peace, and never let me forget that waiting should be a pleasure when I am waiting to see what your hand will reveal. Amen.

Those who wait on the Lord will never be disappointed.

Wings of Light

Wings of light surround me,
And I am enlightened.
Wings of love enfold me,
And I am comforted.
Angels guide my journey,
And I am directed.
Angels keep me safe from harm,
And I am protected.

Arms so strong lift me,
And I am emboldened.
Arms so soft hold me,
And I am at peace.
Angels grant me mercy,
And I am redeemed.
Angels walk beside me,
And I am esteemed.

Songs of joy fill me,
And I am enchanted.
Songs of love envelop me,
And I am empowered.
Angels sing above me,
And I am adored.
Angels chant in glory,
And I am restored.

Send Me an Angel

With upright heart he tended them,
and guided them with skillful hand.

Psalm 78:72

Send me an angel
To help me through my day,
For I don't think that I can take
The challenges that come my way.

I need a winged helper
To lift me from my cares
And pull me up into the light
When I'm drowning in my fears.

Give me a guardian
To hold me while I sleep
And shelter me from any harm
In mighty arms my soul to keep.

Grant me a companion
With strength to carry me along,
To give me hope when I am lost
And teach me right from wrong.

Deliver me an angel
Made especially for me,
One who'll know my deepest dreams
And guide me toward my destiny.

*In the company of angels, every problem
has a solution, every challenge has a
lesson, every cloud has a silver lining.
In the company of angels, troubles are
diminished, trials are overcome, and life
becomes a blessing again.*

Recognizing
His Presence

*May the God of hope fill you with all joy
and peace as you trust in him, so that you
may overflow with hope by the power of the
Holy Spirit.*

Roman 15:13

*A*lleluia, Lord! How we praise you
with our words, our songs, and
our lives! When we look back over all the
situations you've brought us through,
we are so grateful. We are filled with
confidence that we can face the future
because you will be there with us. And
so we just want to stop today and
praise you for all you are and all you do.
Alleluia and Amen!

What I Really Need

Behold the fowls of the air: for they sow not, neither do they reap, nor gather into barns; yet your heavenly Father feedeth them. Are ye not much better than they?

Matthew 6:26 KJV

Lord, help me resist accusing you of being untrue when I don't get from you everything I want, for I know you have promised to meet all my needs. And when I learn to love you supremely and trust you wholly, my desires will find fulfillment in you.

Mercy is not something we need to beg for, since God's pleasure is to love us.

Messengers of God

*And the angel said unto them, Fear not:
for, behold, I bring you good tidings of
great joy, which shall be to all people.*

Luke 2:10 KJV

In the Bible, angels appear to a variety of people with messages appropriate to the people and their situations. If an angel were to come to you today, what message do you think you would receive?

You are truly blessed.
The Lord is with you.
Don't be afraid!

*To receive grace means that we are given
good things in this life, such as angels,
whether we deserve them or not.*

Someone to Watch Over Me

The Lord will guide you continually, and satisfy your needs in parched places, and make your bones strong; and you shall be like a watered garden, like a spring of water, whose waters never fail.

Isaiah 58:11

Thank you for the unseen hands that guide my way. Thank you for the eyes that watch my step. Thank you for the care that keeps me safe, even when the angels are incognito. Thank you for the trouble I have missed even though I never saw it coming. Every visible thing in the world is under the charge of an angel.

—Augustine of Hippo

To Serve and Protect

For the Lord loves justice and fairness;
he will never abandon his people.
They will be kept safe forever;
but all who love wickedness shall perish.

Psalm 37:28 TLB

Dear God,
Thank you for those persons in uniform who watch over us and care for us. Every day, they put their lives on the line to protect, serve, and help complete strangers. Bless them, guide them in their duties, and keep them safe.

Lead the Way!

Consider what I say; and the Lord give thee understanding in all things.

2 Timothy 2:7 KJV

*C*reator of all that exists, come to me as you have come to so many—in the guise of angels. Speak to me your message. Open my ears that I might hear your words. And give me understanding of what you would have me do.

Here I stand at a crossroads,
Wondering which way I should go
I ask for a sign, but in my heart,
I believe I already know.
Intuition? Inspiration? No.
My angel told me so.

All Creatures
Great and Small

*... ask the animals, and they will teach you;
the birds of the air, and they will tell you....
Who among all these does not know that
the hand of the Lord has done this? In his
hand is the life of every living thing and
the breath of every human being.*

Job 12:7, 9–10

God of all things, we thank you
for all your creatures—from the
largest to the smallest. In each of these
wondrous animals, we see your creative
touch. Protect their lives, and help us
respect all you have created. Let us also
be ready to learn from them anything
you would like to teach us.

Minister to My Spirit

The Lord is good to those who wait
for him, to the soul that seeks him.
It is good that one should wait quietly for
the salvation of the Lord.

Lamentations 3:25–26

Lord, help me keep my heart open
to the messengers of your love
that you send my way. Through them,
you minister to my needs—physical,
emotional, mental, and spiritual. Remind
me that each one is an angel—a gift from
your heart, intended to lift and support
me along my way.

Listen for God's Voice

*L*ord, you come to us in the storm, the fire, and even in the stillness of a quiet moment. Sometimes your message is strong, carried on bustling angelic wings. Sometimes our spirits are nudged, our hearts lightened by the gentle whisper of angel voices. However you approach us, your message is always one of tender love and compassion. Thank you for the certainty—and the surprise— of your holy voice.

May you always experience the presence of angels in your daily life so that you may have peace, comfort, and hope for the future.

Travel Companions

Whenever you take a journey—whether across town to a familiar destination or across the country to a new place—remember to take an angel with you. The angel will guide your path, watch your steps, and keep you company along the way.

We never travel alone.
Invisible angels surround us,
walking with us on our journey,
quietly sustaining our spirits and pouring
love over us with the lightness of air.
And we don't even hear
the rustling of their wings.

Shine a Light

The Lord is near to all who call on him....
He fulfills the desire of all who fear him;
he also hears their cry, and saves them.
The Lord watches over all who love him ...

Psalm 145:18–20

Dear God, I need a host of angels to pull me out of this swamp of sorrow and the unrelenting darkness of grief. Please send your angels to shine their light on the beauty of your creation so I can have a few moments of joy today. Tomorrow may be easier, but I really do need as many angels as you can spare today. Thank you. Amen.

Angels help lead us out
of darkness and into God's light.

Always by My Side

"Because he loves me," says the Lord,
"I will rescue him; I will protect him,
for he acknowledges my name.
He will call on me, and I will answer him;
I will be with him in trouble,
I will deliver him and honor him."

Psalm 91:14–15 NIV

Heavenly Father—
I want to thank you for the angels who are always there for me in times of trouble, as well as times of joy. I know I can always turn to them to deliver your wisdom and comfort, no matter what is going on in my life. I am so grateful for their blessed presence, which surrounds me with love and fills me with peace.

83

Your Suffering Servant

*O Lord my God, I cried to you for help,
and you have healed me.*

Psalm 30:2

Father, it's not always clear to
me why suffering comes. But I
do know that whenever I suffer, you
are close at hand. I can see you in the
kindness you deliver to me through your
angels. Some angels are strangers, some
are friends, and some are unseen, but
all remind me that you see me, that you
care for me, and that you are with me.

*Thank you, angels, for all the caring
things you do. Thanks for being so faithful
and seeing me through times of struggle
and despair. I feel more carefree just
knowing you are there.*

A Stormy Path

When life's winds toss me upon the waves of uncertainty and doubt, when the tempest beats me upon rocks of guilt and self-pity, when my pitiful heart yearns for love I cannot find, when the darkness seems darker and the night longer, some unseen hand reaches down, and with a strength and tenderness I cannot comprehend, pulls me back into the light.

Through strife or storm or darkest night,
my angel is there to show me God's light.

Facing Forward

*I consider that the sufferings of this
present time are not worth comparing with
the glory about to be revealed to us.*

Romans 8:18

*L*ord, I treasure my family, for when
things are at their worst, they are
at their best, supporting and loving me
like a band of precious angels sent from
above. I've been dealing with some heavy-
duty challenges lately, but my family is
always there when I need them, and they
always know when I need some quiet
time. With the family you have blessed
me with, I know I can stay focused on

the brighter days ahead and keep my face
turned toward the sun, even when it
seems so dark. My family keeps me real.
Thank you, Lord, for giving them to me.

The future is so much brighter when
you let others help and support you
during your darkest hours.
The people who love you are
servants of God sent to earth
to remind you of how special and
precious you are.

Silently Seeking

*For God alone my soul waits in silence;
from him comes my salvation. He alone is
my rock and my salvation, my fortress; I
shall never be shaken.*

Psalm 62:1–2

O Lord, it occurs to me that at those times when I don't feel your presence or guidance in my life, I may have been creating so much chaos that you couldn't be heard over the din! Calm my anxious heart, Lord. Today, may I take the time to quiet the noise in my life so that I might not miss a single message you want me to hear. I will seek you in the silence of my soul, Lord. Thank you in advance for speaking to me there. Amen.

Never Too Late

Thou art the God that doest wonders: thou hast declared thy strength among the people.

Psalm 77:14 KJV

Regardless of what the future holds, I'm savoring all sorts of wondrous things I've been too busy to notice before. A thousand daily marvels bring a smile to my face. Through your grace, Lord, rather than thinking how sad it is that I missed them before, I'm delighted to be seeing, doing them now. These small wonders energize me, and for that I'm thankful. It's never too late to be a joyful explorer. I really needed you to show me your glory today. Thank you.

Applying to Be an Angel

For this reason . . . we have not stopped
praying for you. We continually ask God to
fill you with the knowledge of his will through
all the wisdom and understanding . . .

Colossians 1:9 NIV

God, I want to be an angel, but I'm
not sure I fit the job description. I
may not even meet the requirements to
get hired. You may have plenty of others
who could do the job better than me.
But my heart is willing, and I can easily
muster enthusiasm for the task ahead. I
know you can work in me, so I'm asking
for your spirit of encouragement—your
special blessing. Help me act like an angel
and ask for no reward. Let your spirit be
my spirit so we can fly together!

My Aha Moment

Dear friends, let us practice loving each other, for love comes from God and those who are loving and kind show that they are the children of God, and that they are getting to know him better. But if a person isn't loving and kind, it shows that he doesn't know God—for God is love.

1 John 4:7–8 TLB

Lord, I think I finally get it. You invest your spirit in me so that I can offer you to the world around me. Help me do this well. My hands and my heart are available to you even if I don't have wings and a halo.

Shared Blessings

*Don't forget to do good and to share what
you have with those in need, for such
sacrifices are very pleasing to him.*

Hebrews 13:16 TLB

Dear God, please be with all the
homeless people and animals,
those struggling with depression or
addiction or loneliness, and those who
are walking through life in a daze, not
as happy as they could be. Send angels
to guide them along life's journey. Please
help them get whatever it is they need
each and every day, whether it's food,
shelter, clean drinking water, a job, a
home, or a loving, supportive network of
family and friends. Please let them always

be treated with the love, compassion, dignity, and respect that they deserve. And please point them in the right direction to get the help they need to feel the love and joy that you want all your children to experience. Thank you. Amen.

Angels look for the best in us and then they nourish that place. They see a vision of whom God has created us to be and they dream that dream with us.

93

There's an Angel in All of Us

Dear brothers and sisters…Be joyful.
Grow to maturity. Encourage each other.
Live in harmony and peace. Then the God
of love and peace will be with you.

2 Corinthians 13:11 NLT

An angel reached out and took my finger today and squeezed it as tight as a baby can squeeze. An angel smiled at me from her wheelchair. An angel sheltered me from the rain and helped me get into the office without getting wet. You may call them a baby, a senior citizen, or a good Samaritan, but they are the angels that watch out for me every day, making my life more comfortable and my awareness more real.

God's Majestic Creations

How many are your works, Lord!
In wisdom you made them all;
the earth is full of your creatures.

Psalm 104:24 NIV

Father God, the earth is asleep. The buds of spring lie in wait. The wonder of your world seems to be in a holding pattern, just waiting for the go-ahead to grow. Let winter teach us the value of stillness, silence, and meditation. Help us know that angel wings don't have to flutter wildly to do the work of your kingdom of peace.

Living in Gratitude

*The Lord, your God, is in your midst, a
warrior who gives victory; he will rejoice
over you with gladness, he will renew you
in his love; he will exult over you with loud
singing as on a day of festival.*

Zephaniah 3:17–18

God, when I least expected it today,
you sent me an angel in the form
of a caring stranger who made my day a
little brighter and a little warmer. It was
nothing big—just a pleasant smile and
some small talk that reminded me that
friendly people are everywhere and that
I may learn something from a random

conversation with someone I've never met before. I am amazed at your consistent and persistent miracles, big and small. If I don't say thank you enough, please forgive me, God. I truly am grateful!

Miracles can be found in every corner if we have the grateful eyes to see them. When we live in a state of gratitude, we are rewarded with more and more things to be grateful for.

I Thought I Met an Angel

I thought I heard an angel
Whisper in my ear,
Telling me which way to go
And that she'd guide me there.

I thought I felt a wisp of a wing
Brush against my arm,
Surrounding me with loving grace
To keep me safe from harm.

I thought I saw an angel
Dancing through the air,
Spreading joy to all below
Who called to God in prayer.

I thought I met an angel
In a loving, caring friend,
There for me through thick and thin,
Loyal 'til the end.

I thought I touched an angel
In the arms of one I love,
Enfolded in the gentle glow
Of blessings from above.

A Compassionate Heart

But love your enemies, do good, and lend,
expecting nothing in return. Your reward
will be great, and you will be children
of the Most High; for he is kind to the
ungrateful and the wicked. Be merciful,
just as your Father is merciful.

Luke 6:35–36

Never let my needs overshadow
my recognition of the needs
of others. Ground me in empathy.
Commission my sympathy. Urge me
to offer comforting hands and an
understanding heart. And in so doing,
show me how easing the pain of others
eases my own.

Actions Speak Louder than Words

Do to others as you would have them do to you.

Luke 6:31 NIV

Heavenly Father, it's easy to say, "Let me know if there's anything I can do." But it is much better to peer closer, assess the situation to find what needs doing, and then simply do it. Help me look into a friend's needs instead of waiting to be asked. Help me replace the words I utter so glibly with actions that might matter even more. Amen.

I Can Do That

When someone needs a favor
Or a shoulder they can cry on,
A kind word of support
Or a friend they can rely on,
I can do that.

When someone needs a helping hand
Or a bit of kind advice,
A confidante to share their dreams
Or just someone who's nice,
I can do that.

When someone cannot carry on
And I have strength to spare,
Or if they're feeling lonely
And they need someone to care,
I can do that.

When someone is afraid
And they see little hope in sight,
Or if they lose their way
And need to find a guiding light,
I can do that.

I can be an angel
To a soul in need today
Or make the going easier
For someone else's way.

Everyone who performs a good deed is
truly an angel. One doesn't need to wear
feathered wings or golden halos to offer a
heavenly helping hand.

Your Ways
Are My Ways

Make me to know your ways, O Lord;
teach me your paths. Lead me in your
truth, and teach me, for you are
the God of my salvation; for you
I wait all day long.

Psalm 25:4–5

Lord, I thank you for the teachers you have sent into my life. Some have hurt me and some have helped me, but all have been instrumental in making me who I am today. I believe they are all angels sent to challenge me to think in higher ways and live a more authentic life. Even those people whom I have felt anger toward have left me with lessons that have helped me to grow and become a more kind and loving person. I thank you for using others as my earthbound angels to help me be the best I can be.

Every person who graces our lives has something to offer. Some may offer lessons, some may just be blessings, but all are angels sent to make us more than we were before.

You Light Up My Life

Let love be genuine…
love one another with mutual affection;
outdo one another in showing honor.

Romans 12:9–10

I've been blessed with a love so deep and true. My husband—my best friend, companion, and angel—is always by my side on the path of life. Thank you, God, for bringing into my world a light and a love so wonderful. Help me to always treat this person with compassion, warmth, and kindness so that our love will last a lifetime. I know people don't always get the chance to marry their best friend, but you have given me that chance, and I hope to never squander it. Help me be the best wife I can be and to always do my share of the loving and giving.

*Finding a true soul mate is like having
your own special angel to walk
life's path with.*

Compassion for Others

*We who are strong ought to put up with
the failings of the weak, and not to please
ourselves. For Christ did not please himself;
but, as it is written, "The insults of those
who insult you have fallen on me."*

Romans 15:1, 3

Father, you have always showed
us how to love the stranger, to
withhold judgment, to help the ungodly,
and to bear the weaknesses of others.
Your son kept company with outcasts and
took on their burdens.

Stir up in us, Lord, your compassion, and
help us to understand this truth: We are
our brother's keepers.

Angels in Disguise

In this day and age, angels are more likely to appear in street clothes than in long white robes and halos. A neighbor who offers sound advice, a mentor who shows us how to live well, a friend who comforts us—all may be angels. If we are open to the possibility that God will use those around us to guide our way, then we may benefit from the direction our earthly angels give. We may not hear harps playing, but in hindsight, we may give thanks for God's angels on earth.

Not all angels are in disguise. Look closer. You might recognize someone you know.

Just Listen

You must understand this, my beloved: let
everyone be quick to listen, slow to speak.

James 1:19

*L*istening is an art that you have
perfected, Lord. Let me, too,
be quick to listen and slow to speak.
Listening shows my friends and family
that I care—that their feelings are
important to me. I pray that I can be the
kind of listener that they need. O loving
Father, help me to listen carefully so I can
help them heal and grow strong. Amen.

People think listening is doing nothing.
But listening—real listening—is hard work
that takes place in the mind.

Simple Faith

"There are no such things as angels,"
Say educated minds,
Those who have the eyes to see
But to the truth are blind.

"There are no such things as angels,"
Say the learned and the wise,
And all those who see the world
Through jaded, skeptical eyes.

"There are no such things as angels,"
The pragmatist replies
As well as the doubting masses
Who on intellect rely.

But I believe in angels
And in miracles and love,
All it takes is simple faith
And blessings from above.

Let Me Hear Your Message

But don't just listen to God's word. You must do what it says. Otherwise, you are only fooling yourselves.

James 1:22 NLT

God of all words and of the angels, I kneel before you in wonder at the ways you speak to me. Help me hear your message in words, in deeds, in thoughts, in relationships, and in nature. Let me, in all things and at all times, be open to your message for my life.

Angels carry messages from heaven to earth. God uses his angels to tell us of his mercy and to show us where he wants us to go.

Angels of Comfort

And the angel of the Lord said to her,
"…the Lord has given heed to your
affliction."

Genesis 16:11

Our hearts are bruised, Father—black and blue from life's pounding, swollen and sore from hurts real and imagined. We need a soothing balm to ease our discomfort. Please send into our lives angelic beings who have healing hands and helping hearts, those who would ease our pain by word and deed. Amen.

No heart is so heavy and no soul is
so bleak that they can't be lifted by
the wings of angels.

The Power of Forgiveness

Be gentle and ready to forgive;
never hold grudges. Remember,
the Lord forgave you,
so you must forgive others.

Colossians 3:13 TLB

God, I don't pretend to be perfect.
I make mistakes. I screw up. I say
and do things that hurt other people.
Let my guardian angel walk with me
today and gently remind me to stop and
think about what I am doing and saying
before I act. I know that you forgive me
for my foibles, but I would like the

guidance and patience to stop making so many of them. Let me forgive myself, as well as those who have wronged me, so we can all treat each other with more kindness, compassion, and dignity. Amen.

Angels see us much differently than we see ourselves. We so often concentrate on our weaknesses and our faults. But angels see us from the inside out because they view us through the love of God.

An Abundant Life

"Do not be afraid, little flock,
for it is your Father's good pleasure to
give you the kingdom."

Luke 12:32

*G*od, I just want to take a little time
out from my day to thank you
for the abundance all around me. There
was a time when all I saw was what I
lacked, but you have taught me to see
blessings in everything and angels in
every being I encounter. I am so thankful
to be surrounded by proof of your love
and grace. There are times when I may

not have all I want, but I always have all I need, and that makes me feel safe and loved and at peace. Amen.

To see proof of God's abundance, simply go outside and try to count the blades of grass in a field.

The Blessings
in the Lessons

*"In everything do to others as you would
have them do to you; for this is
the law and the prophets."*

Matthew 7:12

God, I know that we are all created
in your image, so I hope to always
be a positive role model. I know that is
a tall order, so when I fall short, help me
have the same compassion for myself as
I have for those who don't always treat
me properly. Just as others often act as
angels for me, I would like to do the
same for them. Let me be someone else's
wings today.

Some of our most significant teachers come to us in the form of difficult people who press our buttons, vex our spirits, and get on our nerves. But these people act as mirrors to expose the negative traits that we dislike in ourselves. Learn from these people. They are a gift.

Light My Way

For we know that if the earthly tent
we live in is destroyed, we have a building
from God, an eternal house in heaven,
not built by human hands.

2 Corinthians 5:1 NIV

Father, hold us in your arms in
the midst of devastation and
ruin. Remind us that rampaging nature
and human evil will not touch us in
our eternal homes. Send your angels to
remind us that our lives and homes on
earth are part of the journey, not our
final destination. Amen.

*Sometimes hope seems as unreal as
the angel beside you. But both are real.*

Faith Versus Fear

Bless the Lord, ye his angels, that excel
in strength, that do his commandments,
hearkening unto the voice of his word.

Psalm 103:20 KJV

*L*oving Lord, you have sent
angels to your people on earth
throughout history. Some brought
messages of hope, others gave warning.
Some angels helped still fearful hearts
or encourage the downtrodden. Thank
you for always being there.

In the most important moments of
humanity, angels have served as holy
commentators, announcing the good
news of new life and resurrection.
With women and men, angels have
celebrated the wonder of God's redemption.

Refocus My Attention

*Take delight in the Lord, and he will
give you the desires of your heart.*

Psalm 37:4 NIV

Lord, I've been feeling really down lately. Forgive me if I don't seem grateful for all the blessings you bestow on me each and every day. I truly am appreciative, but right now, I'm having a difficult time focusing on what I *do* have rather than the things that I'm longing for. Please let my guardian angels lift me out of these blues and carry me through this dark time. Help them fill me with faith that you will provide for all my heart's desires. Thank you. Amen.

Divine Protection

*L*ord in heaven,
Please help me to see the angels
whom I know you have placed in my
presence. Help me to slow down and
know that I am always divinely protected
and guided. Help me to spread your
word, do your work, be kind, and love.
Thank you, Lord, for your help this day.

*An angel doesn't have to speak
to be heard, be visible to be seen,
or be present to be felt.
Believe in angels
and they will always be near.*

What Really Lasts

Do you want to be truly rich?
You already are if you are happy and good.
After all, we didn't bring any money with
us when we came into the world,
and we can't carry away a single penny
when we die.

1 Timothy 6:6–7 TLB

God, you have blessed me with children who keep my heart light and free. You have blessed me with elderly relatives who provide guidance and understanding, for they have been through every storm that now faces me. You have blessed me with friends who offer shoulders to lean on or cry on, whatever I may need. I am surrounded by angels of every size, color, shape, and age, and I am forever grateful for these amazing treasures you have bestowed upon me. Thank you, God.

When life on earth is ending, people don't surround themselves with objects. What we want around us is people—people we love and have relationships with.

—Rick Warren

Love, 24/7

Therefore, I tell you, her sins, which were many, have been forgiven; hence she has shown great love. But the one to whom little is forgiven, loves little.

Luke 7:47

God, bless the unknown angels who clear the cluttered paths of the lost, who wipe the tears of the grieving, and who hold the hands that tremble in fear. Their names may be known only to you, but their acts of mercy give me the assurance that your love touches everyone, everywhere. Amen.

In Your Hand

But I trust in you, O Lord;
I say, "You are my God."
My times are in your hand.

Psalm 31:14–15

My times are in Thy hand;
My God, I wish them there;
My life, my friends, my soul I leave
Entirely to Thy care.

—William F. Lloyd

Held in the palm of God's hand—
not manipulated by that
hand, not crushed by it,
not entrapped within,
but held tenderly with love,
we find our safest place.

Courage and Strength

*These troubles and sufferings of ours are,
after all, quite small and won't last very
long.... So we do not look at what we
can see right now, the troubles all around
us, but we look forward to the joys in
heaven which we have not yet seen.
The troubles will soon be over, but
the joys to come will last forever.*

2 Corinthians 4:17–18 TLB

You know, Lord, lately I have been struggling just to get through the next hour, the next minute, and the next second. Be merciful to me in my weakness and bring me strength and encouragement through the angels you send. They are faithful messengers of your compassion and comfort. Amen.

Take My Hand

*For all who are led by the Spirit of God
are children of God.*

Romans 8:14

God, I am a child no longer, yet I still know the need to have someone take me by the hand and lead me out of a scary place. Throughout my life, you've sent those people to me, and together we have found the way. Bless those angels, Lord. May they find the hands to hold when they need them. Amen.

If you pray truly, you will feel within yourself a great assurance, and the angels will be your companions.

—Evagrius of Pontus

Angels All Around Us

There are angels all around us,
No one is ever alone,
Even in our darkest hour,
Our deepest needs are known.
There are angels all around us,
Though seldom can we see,
The guardians among us,
Watching over you and me.

There are angels all around us,
Hidden barely out of sight,
Waiting for the moment when
The time to give is right.
If you listen then your heart may hear
The rustle of angel wings
Or catch a glimmer of a halo's glow,
A hint that angels are real things.

There are angels all around us.
They wipe away our tears.
They tend to our breaking hearts,
Our pain, our grief, our fears.
There are angels all around us,
Though we rarely get to see
The angels all around us,
Watching over you and me.

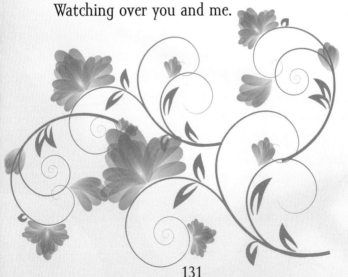

Be a Do-Gooder!

Lord, let me be an angel for someone today. I know how good it feels to have someone do something good for me, and I tend to get so self-involved that I often forget to pay it forward. Help me to find opportunities to be of help to people, no matter how big or small the acts might be. Remind me to smile, hold doors open, and make small talk that we humans seem to do so little of lately. Help me help others remember that we all need each other. The world can be such a cold place; let me spread a little warmth today!

A Friend in Need

I give you a new commandment, that you love one another. Just as I have loved you, you also should love one another.

John 13:34

Dear God,
A special friend of mine is hurting right now. He's going through a difficult time, and he needs encouragement. I pray that you'll heal his aching heart and soothe his soul. May your loving angels guide him in the right direction and pull him out of his grief and sadness. Help him find the happiness and love that he deserves. Please help me always be there for him to laugh and to cry and to offer him love and support.

Finding God in Chaos

From there you will seek the Lord your God, and you will find him if you search after him with all your heart and soul.

Deuteronomy 4:29

Lord, how grateful I am that wherever I find myself I know without a doubt that I will find you there if I open my heart and my eyes to see you. Whatever situation I've gotten myself into, you are there in the midst of it. Too often I forget to look for you within the chaos and confusion, but that doesn't mean you aren't present. Thank you, Lord, for making it possible for me to find you just when I need you most. Amen.

When you can't find God, it isn't God who is lost. Open your heart, close your mouth, and pray.

Our Angels

They flutter, they flicker,
They flash and they fly.
They skim along, soar above,
And sail through the sky.
They dart and they dance,
They dash all around.
They hover and sweep,
Not making a sound.
They plunge and they launch,
They sail like a breeze.
They worship and tremble
And fall on their knees.
They rescue, they liberate,
They guard and preserve.

They give us protection,
They give us the nerve
To stand a bit taller,
To trust a bit more,
To face disappointment
With both feet on the floor,
To revere and to hope
In a place they call home,
To live with the knowledge
That we're never alone.

Someone Else's Angel

Dear friends, since God loved us as much as that, we surely ought to love each other too. For though we have never yet seen God, when we love each other God lives in us and his love within us grows ever stronger.

1 John 4:11–12 TLB

God, with health and financial and relationship issues, I've been so focused on myself and my problems lately that it's no wonder I feel alone, lost, and adrift. I ask that you help me to climb out of myself for a little while and be of help to another. Perhaps by making someone else feel accepted, loved, and cared for, I will be lifted out of my own life just long enough to feel more connected and less alone. Help me see the big picture of this puzzle called my life instead of being so intensely focused on each piece. God, help me to be an angel to others and to relight my own heart in doing so.

If I can put one touch of rosy sunset into the life of any man or woman, I shall feel that I have worked with God.
—G. K. Chesterton

Help in Difficulty

When I thought, "My foot is slipping," your steadfast love, O Lord, held me up. When the cares of my heart are many, your consolations cheer my soul.

Psalm 94:18–19

*L*ord, I need you here in the midst of this difficult situation. I know the very warmth of your love will bring about resolution and that the brightness of your light will cast out all shadows between us. Amen.

Just as each cloud is lined with silver, so, too, is each painful experience lined with the miracle of lessons learned and wisdom gained. God never takes something from us without giving us something else in return.

God's Steadfast Love

O give thanks to the Lord, for he is good,
for his steadfast love endures forever.

Psalm 136:1

God, you love us more than we can ever comprehend. You have even given your angels charge over us, to guide and protect us. Help us be worthy of your love and the angels' care, so that those we meet might consider us bearers of angelic love.

In the mysterious, unexplained events
of our lives, we sense the hand of an
intervening angel to remind us of the
reality of God's ever-present love.

The Child Inside Guides the Way

[Jesus said,] "Truly I tell you, unless you change and become like children, you will never enter the kingdom of heaven. Whoever becomes humble like this child is the greatest in the kingdom of heaven."

Matthew 18:3–4

Dear Lord, help me find the child inside me again. That child is my own inner angel, urging me to slow down and smell the roses. I work so hard for my family and often forget the joy and wonder of just being alive and playing.

Help me to see that joy is the greatest gift and that I don't always have to bury myself in work and obligations to feel that I am a good, worthy person. Bring out the child in me today, Lord, and give me wings. Let me see life through the fresh eyes of awe and wonder again, happy and without a care in the world.

Life is not just about work and making a living. It's about being alive and letting our hearts sing and dance and enjoy the fruits of our labor. Let yourself be merry for a while... the work will always be there.

Doubting No More

But let him ask in faith, nothing wavering.
For he that wavereth is like a wave of the
sea driven with the wind and tossed.

James 1:6 KJV

I see a robin's egg hatching, Lord, and am set free from my doubts and fretting. For, while life is not always filled with joy and happiness, I know it is always held in your hand. Thank you for opening my eyes to your wonders and giving me peace.

Thank you, God, for letting me walk in the
sunshine of your love.

Friendly Reminder

*I was overjoyed when some of the friends
arrived and testified to your faithfulness
to the truth, namely how you walk in the
truth.*

3 John 1:3

Although my eyes should always
be turned above toward God,
sometimes I can do with a reminder
of God's work just a little bit closer to
home. The faith of others can serve as a
reminder or an inspiration to strengthen
my own faith. Just as I should provide
encouragement to others, I can draw on
others to help steady myself.

*Other believers can provide me with God's
guidance if I only remember to look.*

Angels of Hope and Faith

Be glad for all God is planning for you.
Be patient... and prayerful always.

Romans 12:12 TLB

Lord, thank you for blessing me with angels who have taught me to have faith and hope and to trust in your will and your timing. It's not always easy to be patient or to relinquish control, but I'm grateful that you've allowed me to put my worries and desires in your hands, trusting that you know what's best for me. Thank you to my angels for taking my hand and guiding me each step of the way.

A Prayer for Healing

*In my desperation I prayed, and the Lord
listened; he saved me from all my troubles.
For the angel of the Lord is a guard; he
surrounds and defends all who fear him.*

Psalm 34:6–7 NLT

Lord, you made me; you can fix me. You put my body together. You knitted my nerves. You wrote my DNA. You taught me how to laugh and how to love. Something's wrong now—the system's crashing. I trust you to make it better. But what does "better" mean? Healthy, yes, but also whole again. Body, mind, feelings in balance, relationships in sync, my spirit soaring with yours. Lord, you created me and called your creation good. Make me whole again, please. Amen.

Superpowers Activate!

The Lord is the everlasting God, the Creator of the ends of the earth.... He gives power to the faint, and strengthens the powerless.... those who wait for the Lord shall renew their strength,... they shall run and not be weary, they shall walk and not faint.

Isaiah 40:28–29, 31

God, sometimes I feel like a superhero. Taking care of a family, working for a living, fixing this boo-boo, solving that problem, and trying to find time for myself has me feeling like I should be wearing wings or a cape. Help me rise to the occasion of being an amazing angel and hero for others when I can. And also help me find quiet time for myself so I can get up and do it all again tomorrow. Keep me focused on what counts and strong enough to overcome the little things that zap my energy and spirit so I can handle the bigger things. I know others count on me, but I can only do so much without your help.

God will always step in and do for us what we cannot do for ourselves.

Seeking God in the Sacred

Ascribe to the Lord the glory due his name;
bring an offering, and come before him.

1 Chronicles 16:29

Almighty God, thank you for filling our world with glimpses of your holiness. In so many ways you surprise me with the sacred! When I am awake and aware of your presence in our world, I see the holiness evident in an ordinary day: the sunlight across the floor, the kindness of a stranger, a smile from a child. All that is good and righteous, all that is holy, comes from you, O God. May I never miss a moment of it.

There is enough holiness in an ordinary day to make the angels sing!

In God's Hands

And this is my prayer, that your love
may overflow more and more
with knowledge and full insight to
help you to determine what is best.

Philippians 1:9–10

*L*ord, how I pray for the young people I love as they head out into the world on their own. Help them tune in to your presence, Lord, and make them wise beyond their years. Warn them of dangers and protect them from the schemes of others. Teach them to love themselves and others extravagantly, but wisely as well. They are your children, Lord, and you love them even more than I do. I place them in your hands.

Friends Are Worry Erasers

Don't worry about anything; instead, pray about everything; tell God your needs and don't forget to thank him for his answers. If you do this you will experience God's peace, which is far more wonderful than the human mind can understand. His peace will keep your thoughts and your hearts quiet and at rest as you trust in Christ Jesus.

Philippians 4:6–7 TLB

*G*od, when my heart is filled with worry, you never fail to send a friend into my life to lift my spirits. Whether it's an email with a funny picture, a phone call, or a visit for coffee, my friends always seem to know when I need their love and presence the most. True friends are angels in disguise, and I am so thankful for the old and new friends you have sent to help me when I most need a little extra light. I pray I will always be there for them when they need me as well.

Nothing helps alleviate worry better than a visit from a supportive and caring friend who knows just what to say and do to make you feel on top of the world again.

Law of the Lord

*Happy are those who do not follow
the advice of the wicked, or take the path
that sinners tread, or sit in the seat
of scoffers; but their delight is in
the law of the Lord, and on his law
they meditate day and night.*

Psalm 1:1–2

Dear Lord, if I am to succeed meaningfully in this life, I must succeed first in being a person rich in integrity and love. Only then will all other successes find their significance. I know this is true because you've told me this so many times in the past. Please continue to help me be the person you want me to be. Amen.

Be My Guide

The people who walked in darkness
have seen a great light; those who lived
in a land of deep darkness—on them
light has shined.

Isaiah 9:2

Excuse me, God, but it's pretty dark in here right now. If it's not too much trouble, I could sure use an angel or two to help me see what's going on. Just a little help to get me moving in the right direction would be so very much appreciated. I know the dawn is coming. I'm just not sure which direction to turn to find it. Thanks!

When it's too dark to see your path,
trust your angels to guide you.

Being Willing

Wait on the Lord: be of good courage,
and he shall strengthen thine heart:
wait, I say, on the Lord.

Psalm 27:14 KJV

It's hard, Lord, to reveal my heart
to you, though it's the thing I most
want to do. Remind me in this dialogue
that you already know what is within
me. You wait—O thank you!—hoping for
the gift of my willingness to acknowledge
the good you already see and the bad
you've long forgotten.

A Prayer About Angels

Lord, open my eyes that I might see a whole new level of reality. When I feel overwhelmed by my problems, show me your angelic army all around me. Thank you for the tenacious way they guard me, keeping me from potential harm that I may never even know about. Let me join my voice with theirs in praising you: the holy one, the worthy one, the victor over all in heaven and earth. Glory to you in the highest, Lord, and peace in my little world. Amen.

Faith is to believe what we do not see, and the reward of this faith is to see what we believe.

—Augustine of Hippo

Hear Me, O God

You hear, O Lord, the desire of the
afflicted; you encourage them, and you
listen to their cry.

Psalm 10:17 NIV

God hears my cries for help, and
He answers every prayer.
I only need be patient—
He supplies the "how" and "where."
Sometimes it may be immediate
In a tangible way I'll know;
While other times I wait assured
That he is strengthening my soul.
His grace is all-sufficient
To meet my heart-cries' need.
As I lean upon his promises,
Walking in faith, he'll lead.

Letting Go of the Past

For I know the plans I have for you, says the Lord. They are plans for good and not for evil, to give you a future and a hope.

Jeremiah 29:11 TLB

Dear God,
Thank you for sending your angels to give me the courage and strength to let go of the past so that I could move on with my life and embrace all the amazing things you have planned for me. I'm so grateful that you gave me the power to forgive those who have hurt me in the past so that I could be free to give and receive love with a whole heart. Thank you for being patient with me. Amen.

Acknowledgments:

Unless otherwise noted, all scripture quotations are taken from the *New Revised Standard Version* of the Bible. Copyright © 1989 by the Division of Christian Education of the National Council of the Churches of Christ in the United States of America. Used by permission. All rights reserved.

Scripture quotations marked KJV are taken from *The Holy Bible, King James Version*. Copyright © 1977, 1984, Thomas Nelson Inc., Publishers.

Scripture quotations marked NIV are taken from *The Holy Bible, New International Version®*, NIV®. Copyright © 1973, 1978, 1984, 2011 by Biblica, Inc.™ Used by permission of Zondervan. All rights reserved worldwide.

Scripture quotations marked NLT are taken from *The Holy Bible, New Living Translation*, copyright © 1996, 2004, 2007 by Tyndale House Foundation. Used by permission of Tyndale House Publishers, Inc., Carol Stream, Illinois, 60188. All rights reserved.

Scripture quotations marked TLB are taken from *The Living Bible*, copyright © 1971. Used by permission of Tyndale House Publishers, Inc., Carol Stream, Illinois, 60188. All rights reserved.